# Best Jokes & Riddles

Compiled by Anna Pansini
Illustrated by Carolyn Loh

**Troll Associates**

A TROLL BOOK, published by Troll Associates,
Mahwah, NJ 07430

Copyright © 1990 by Troll Associates, Mahwah, New Jersey

Printed in the United States of America.

10  9  8  7  6  5  4  3

# What Makes You Laugh?

When we asked kids across America to send in their favorite jokes for Troll's **Great Giggle and Riddle Contest,** the response was incredible! Riddles, knock-knock jokes, funny lines about monsters, animals, and ghosts—thousands of zany jokes from kids came pouring in.

The result of the contest is two terrific books— this one, and a companion book called *Great Riddles, Giggles & Jokes.* They're each filled with 350 of *your* best jokes.

The contestant's name appears under each joke. (When we received duplicate jokes, we chose the earliest entry.) Both books contain an alphabetical listing of winners, along with their age or grade, school, and school address.

Finally, we'd like to thank all the children who entered the contest, and the teachers who encouraged them.

# Classroom Capers

Teacher: Tim, what did you write your report on?
Tim: A piece of paper.

*James Sunny*

Father: What did you learn in school today?
Daughter: My teacher taught us writing.
Father: What did you write?
Daughter: I don't know. She hasn't taught us reading yet.

*Cindy Garrison*

Teacher: Who can tell me where the English Channel is?
Jane: I don't know. It's not on my TV.

*Lorena S. Pecson*

**Why do teachers take aspirin?**
For de-tension headaches.

*Andy Symonds*

Student: Teacher, I can't do this problem.
Teacher: Any six-year-old should be able to do it.
Student: Well, no wonder I can't. I'm ten.

*Lisa Frohnheiser*

Teacher: Bobby, if I have two sandwiches and you have two sandwiches, what do we have?
Bobby: LUNCH!

*Anthony Santoli*

Teacher: What is your favorite state, Sam?
Sam: Mississippi.
Teacher: How do you spell it?
Sam: Er... I like Ohio much better.

*Katie Callan*

First Person: How did you do on your history exam?
Second Person: Not very well, but it wasn't my fault. They asked me about things that happened before I was born.

*Jonas Young*

Teacher: What's the chemical formula for water?
Student: H, i, j, k, l, m, n, o.
Teacher: May I ask what that is?
Student: That's what you said last week, "Water is H to O."

*Aaron Mangabang*

Principal: Young man, I have to say you're different from the rest of the students.
Student: Really!
Principal: Yes, they're graduating.

*Tommy Arbour*


George: There was a riot in the library.
Kyle: What happened?
George: Somebody found "dynamite" in the dictionary.

*Joshua M. Sheehan*


Teacher: Why are you writing that letter so slowly?
Student: Because it's to my sister, and she can't read fast.

*Joy Fike*


Mother: What did you learn in school today?
Daughter: How to talk without moving my lips.

*Holly Kobolt*


Phil: Jack, what smells in the lunchroom?
Jack: I don't know.
Phil: Your nose!

*April Gobel*


First Student: Were the test questions easy?
Second Student: The questions were easy. The answers were hard.

*AnnMarie Podobinski*


Teacher: How did you get that horrible swelling on your nose?
Scott: I bent over to smell a brose.
Teacher: There's no B in rose.
Scott: There was in this one.

*Jessica Schmelzer*


Teacher: Put the words "detail," "defeat" and "defense" in a sentence.
Student: I already have mine.
Teacher: Okay, read it.
Student: Defeat of de fox went over defense before detail.

*Amy Heineke*


Teacher: Why do we sometimes call the Middle Ages the Dark Ages?
Polly: Because there were so many knights.

*Taylor Strait*

5

# It's Raining Riddles

**Why did Tarzan lose the tennis match?**
Because he was playing against a cheetah.

*Cheryl Connors*

**Why is it always cool in sports arenas?**
Because there's a fan in every seat.

*Charley McCleary*

**What does a frog do at a baseball game?**
He catches all the flies.

*Conor Moore*

**Why was Cinderella thrown off the baseball team?**
Because she ran away from the ball.

*David Malaythong*

**When do baseball players wear armor?**
During knight games.

*Rocio Plata*

**Why did the skeleton cross the road?**
To get to the body shop.

*Matt Enderby*

**Who plays when he works, and works hard when he plays?**
A one-man band.

*Stefanie Stombres*

**Why is it a bad idea to do math problems in the jungle?**
Because if you add 4 + 4, you get ate (8).

*Laura Friese*

**What weighs almost nothing, but can't be held for long?**
Your breath.

*Jimmy Cunat*

**What comes once in a minute, twice in a moment, and never in a thousand years?**
The letter M.

*Liam E. Harrison*

**What has 12 tails, one horn, and squeals?**
A dozen pigs in a livestock truck.

*Vanessa Galati*

**If you had 10 pounds of feathers and 10 pounds of bricks, which would weigh more?**
Neither, they both weigh the same.

*Libby Wasilchuk*

**It's a dark, freezing cold night. You have been wandering in a blizzard for a day and a half. You spot a log cabin. You go in it and see a wood-burning stove, a kerosene lamp, an oil burner, and one candle. You only have one match. What do you light first?**
The match.

*John Smythe*

**What is worse than a giraffe with a sore throat?**
A centipede with sore feet.

*David Reding*

**What has teeth but doesn't bite?**
A comb.

*Travis Lee*

**What has four legs and flies?**
A picnic table.

*Allison Madonna*

**What has many leaves but no branches?**
A book.

*Tommie Denlinger*

**What word becomes shorter when you add two letters to it?**
*Short.* Add "er" and it becomes shorter.

*Nicholas Santone*

**Why is it useless to send a letter to Washington?**
Because he died in 1799.

*Brenda Lieb*

# Nutty Knock-Knocks

Knock! Knock!
Who's there?
Horn.
Horn who?
Horn go beep, beep; car go varoom!

*Chris Brown*

Knock! Knock!
Who's there?
Harry.
Harry who?
Harry up and let me in.

*Andrew Fraerman*

Knock! Knock!
Who's there?
Alma.
Alma who?
Alma cookies are gone and I want more.

*Andrea Arrigo*

Knock! Knock!
Who's there?
Orange.
Orange who?
Orange you gonna come and open the door?

*Jessica Molinares*

Knock! Knock!
Who's there?
Dishes.
Dishes who?
Dishes your friend, open the door.
*Denece Hall*

Knock! Knock!
Who's there?
Oswald.
Oswald who?
Oswald my bubble gum.
*Jodi Furnival*

8

Knock! Knock!
Who's there?
Bear.
Bear who?
Bear with me. I forgot the rest of the joke.
*Tabitha Sadowski*

Knock! Knock!
Who's there?
Justin.
Justin who?
Justin time for dinner.
*Jason Shelton*

Knock! Knock!
Who's there?
Dwayne.
Dwayne who?
Dwayne the bathtub, I'm drowning.

*Stephanie DeLano*

Knock! Knock!
Who's there?
Ben.
Ben who?
Ben looking all over for you.
*Danny Nieken*

Knock! Knock!
Who's there?
Jaws.
Jaws who?
Jaws truly.

*Matt McClendon*

Knock! Knock!
Who's there?
Arthur.
Arthur who?
Arthur any more cookies in the cookie jar?

*Haley Dean Tycer*

Knock! Knock!
Who's there?
Diploma.
Diploma who?
Diploma has come to fix your faucet.

*Robert Hines* 9

# Riddle Dee-Dee

**What's green and white and goes 125 miles an hour?**
A frog in a white racing car.

*Jeremy Barb*

**When is a piece of string like a piece of wood?**
When it has knots in it.

*Nikki Evanush*

**What is just as big as you but doesn't weigh a single pound?**
Your shadow.

*Cindy Wilson*

**Why is a bride unlucky on her wedding day?**
Because she's not marrying the best man.

*Nichole DeLaire*

**Two men stand at the same fork in the road. One man always lies and the other man always tells the truth, but you don't know which man is which. They can talk to each other, but you can only talk to one of the men. What question will you ask, and which man should you ask it of in order to find out the correct road to follow?**
You can ask either man, "Which way will the other man tell me to go?" You should then go the opposite way because the honest man will tell you what road the liar would tell you to take, which would not be the correct way; and the liar would tell you what road the honest man would not tell you to take, which would not be the correct road.

*April Bree Bullock*

**I can make words disappear and the more you use me, the smaller I become. What am I?**
An eraser.

*Erica Dattilio*

**Did you hear the joke about the bed?**
It hasn't been made up yet.

*Donald Moyer*

**Why did the chicken cross the park?**
To get to the other slide.

*David Bonarigo*

**What's black and white and red all over?**
A zebra with the measles.

10

*Eric Day*

# Space Solos

**How does the man in the moon cut his hair?**
Eclipse it!

*Steven Ciregna*

**When is the moon going broke?**
When it's down to its last quarter.
*Marlena Russell*

**How do Martians shave?**
With laser blades.

*Mike Butala*

**Did you hear about the new restaurant on the moon?**
Great food, but no atmosphere.
*Lucilla Dagostino*

**What was the first animal in space?**
The cow. It jumped over the moon.
*Jessicah Gallagher*

A very far-out looking alien from Mars went to the doctor. After the examination the doctor said, "I'm very sorry but you have heart trouble." The alien replied, "I want a second opinion." The doctor said, "Okay. You're ugly too."

*Rebecca Bledsoe*

**What do you do to get ready for an astronaut's birthday party?**
You plan-et.

*Brian Pruitt*

Sue: Did you know the astronauts found some bones on the moon?
Betty: Oh, dear! I guess the cow didn't make it over after all.
*Shane Siewert*

**Which planet is like a circus?**
Saturn, because it has 3 rings.

*Megan Lantz*

Once there was an alien that came from outer space. He landed on Earth near a baby chick. He asked the chick, "Is there a hotel around here?" The chick said, "Cheep! Cheep!" "I hope it is," said the alien. "Getting here cost me a fortune."

*Sarah Lloyd* 11

# In the Mood for Food

How do you pay compliments to bread?
You toast it.

*Emily Baldwin*

What is a cheerleader's favorite soft drink?
Root beer.

*Stacey Rivenburg*

What can't you have for breakfast?
Lunch and dinner.

*Sara Minster*

Why are bananas so popular?
Because they have a-peel.

*Christine Bowen*

Why is honey scarce in Boston?
Because there's only one B in Boston.

*Jesse Hallowell*

Why did the tomato blush?
Because it saw the salad dressing.
*Rachna Chandiramani*

What do computers eat for a snack?
Micro chips.

*Theresa Link*

Why did the potato go to France?
Because it wanted to be a French fry.
*Lauren Esposito*

What kind of shoes do you make out of banana skins?
Slippers.

*Stacie Caris*

Why did the raisin ask the fig out?
Because he couldn't find a date.
*Michael Rivera*

How does a hungry man eat a hot dog?
With relish.
*Daniel Wright*

**Where was the first French fry made?**
In Greece.

*Robert Winkel*

**Why aren't lemons allowed to sing or play music?**
Because they hit too many sour notes.
*Jennifer Sprouse*

**How do you keep milk from going bad?**
Leave it in the cow.
*Jenny Campanaro*

**If a pickle is one year old,
what should you do?**
Wish it "Happy Birthday."
*Joleen Tolman*

**Can a hamburger run a mile in under 4 minutes?**
Yes, because it's fast food.

*Danny Hushagen*

**Who leads the popcorn?**
The kernel.
*Penny Frederickson*

*Attention!*

**What kind of meat do you get from
a cow with 2 short legs and 2 long legs?**
Lean meat.
*Elisha Winston*

**What is the best thing to put into a pie?**
Your teeth.

*Kimberly Stewert*

**What happens when a banana sees a ghost?**
The banana splits.

*Judy Wang*

**How do you make a strawberry shake?**
Take it to a horror movie.

*Cindy Hunter*

**Which fruits are never lonely?**
Bananas and grapes because they hang around in bunches.
*Thomas Richard Puffer*

13

# Did You Hear That?

**What did one elevator say to the other elevator?**
"I think I'm coming down with something."

*Tonetta Norman*

**What did the hat say to the coat hanger?**
"You stay here while I go on a head."

*Thomas Smith*

**What did one sandwich say to the other sandwich?**
"You're full of bologna."

*Dan Muskie*

**What did the duck say when it went shopping?**
"Put it on my bill."

*Jennifer Tucci*

**What did one rose say to the other?**
"Hi, bud."

*Josh Sloan*

**What did the digital watch say to the grandmother clock?**
"Look, Ma! No hands!"

*Amanda Church*

**What do birds say on Halloween?**
"Trick or tweet?"

*Rebecca Scheffy*

**What did the porcupine say to the cactus?**
"Is that you, Mama?"

*Jonathan Kendrick*

**What do frogs say on the first day of January?**
"Have a Hoppy New Year!"

*Derron Jones*

**What did the banana say to the dog?**
Nothing, bananas can't talk.

*Ryan Horvath*

**What did the candle say to the other candle?**
"Don't birthdays burn you up?"

*Kathryn Wood*

14

**What did the math book say to the reading book?**
"I bet I have more problems than you."

*Raquelle Bainter*

**What did the cowboy say when he landed on a cactus?**
"Ouch!"

*Joseph Molesky*

**What did the Pink Panther say when he stepped on an ant?**
"Dead ant, dead ant, dead ant, dead ant, dead ant, dead ant."

*Marquist Harris*

**What did the mother rope say to the baby rope?**
"Don't be knotty."

*Matt Tindall*

**What did one book say to the other book?**
"Where are you bound?"

*Angie Taylor*

**What did the truck driver say when he lost his tire?**
"You picked a fine time to leave me loose wheel."

*Gary Powers*

**What did Benjamin Franklin say when he discovered electricity?**
Nothing. He was too shocked.
*Erin McCracken*

**What did one wall say to the other wall?**
"I'll meet you at the corner."

*Andrea Charles*

**What did the rug say to the floor?**
"I've got you covered."

*Jason Wootton*

**What did one penny say to the other penny?**
"Let's get together and make some cents."

*Anna Moser*

15

# How Are You Feeling?

Patient: Doctor, my hair's falling out! Can you give me
    something to keep it in?
Doctor: Sure! How about a paper bag?
         *Kristy McGovern*

**What do you have when your head
is hot, your feet are cold and you
see spots in front of your eyes?**
A polka-dot sock on your head.
         *Bradley Spitzer*

Patient: I haven't been able to sleep lately. Every night, I have
    the same dream. There's a door with a sign on it. I pull and
    pull but the door doesn't open.
Doctor: What does the sign say?
Patient: Push.

         *Nicole Boemi*

First Person: What's the quickest way to get to the hospital?
Second Person: Stand in the middle of a busy street.
         *Jason Feulner*

**What kind of headaches do trees get?**
Tree-mendous headaches.

         *Haddi Falkner*

First Person: I have butterflies in my stomach.
Second Person: Why don't you take an aspirin?
First Person: I did, but now they're playing ping-pong with it.
         *Megan Johnston*

Patient: Doctor, when my hand gets better will I be able to play
    the piano?
Doctor: Of course.
Patient: That's great. I could never play the piano before.
         *Erin Greening*

**If an apple a day keeps the doctor away, what does a garlic
clove do?**
It keeps everyone away.

         *Jennifer Mertz*

**Where do sick boats go?**
To the dock.
    *Christine McCulken*

Patient: Doctor, I feel like a deck of cards.
Doctor: I'll deal with you later.

    *Tara Campbell*

**Why did the house call the doctor?**
Because it had a window pain.

    *Kevin Twomey*

**What kind of water should you drink when you are sick?**
Well water.

    *Carmen Beier*

Patient: Doctor, I think I'm a bullfrog.
Doctor: How long have you thought this?
Patient: Ever since I was a tadpole.

    *Jason van der Linde*

**What should you do when a health specialist knocks at your door?**
Vit'am-in.

    *Kristen McAuliffe*

**Why did the boy take his comb to the dentist?**
Because it lost a tooth.

    *Brandi Wyatt*

**Why was the patient laughing after surgery?**
Because the doctor left him in stitches.
    *Patrick Murphy*

**What did the doctor prescribe
to get rid of the measles?**
Spot remover.
    *Amanda Cumberland*

# Amusing Animals

**What should you do when a bull charges you?**
Pay him.

*Matthew Williams*

Once there was a room full of cats. Cats were everywhere—on chairs, tables, even hanging from lamps. A mama mouse and her three babies went across the floor. All the cats got quiet and formed a line behind the mice. Then, all of a sudden, the mama mouse turned around and said, "BOW-WOW!" And all the cats ran away. Then the mama mouse turned to her babies and said, "It pays to know another language."

*Grady Allen Smith*

**What did the gorilla use to fix the sink?**
A monkey wrench.

*Erik DiNardo*

**What do rabbits have that no other animals have?**
Baby rabbits.

*Leah Kubczak*

**Why don't chickens make good baseball players?**
Because they can only hit fowl balls.

*Wendy Fry*

**Why don't leopards play hide and seek?**
Because they are always spotted.

*Craig Bernotus*

**How do you keep a skunk from smelling?**
Hold its nose.

*Brandon Bulthuis*

**Who does a horse like best?**
Its neigh-bors.

*Allison Rogde*

**Why do monkeys scratch themselves?**
Because they're the only ones who know where it itches.

*Maria Aguirre*

**Why do mother kangaroos hate rainy days?**
Because then their children have to play inside.

*Tricia Lynn Payne*

18

**Why do cows give milk?**
Because they aren't smart enough to sell it.

*Jennifer Warmouth*

**What did the gorilla say when his sister had a baby?**
"Well, I'll be a monkey's uncle."

*Billy Garrett*

**Why did the chicken lay an egg?**
Because if she dropped it, it would break.
*Rusty Miller*

**How do you stop a bull from charging?**
You take away its credit card.
*Wendy Bryson*

**Why do birds fly south for the winter?**
Because it's too far to walk.
*Rachelle Farries*

**How do you catch a squirrel?**
Climb up a tree and act like a nut.
*Sandy Acreman*

**Why couldn't the pony sing?**
Because it was a little hoarse.
*Nathan Morales*

**Why should you never ask a Brontosaurus to tell you a bedtime story?**
Because their tales are very long.

*Ronald Darby*

**Where does a two-ton gorilla sit at the movies?**
Wherever it wants.

*Bryan Hoy*

**What is the first thing baby apes learn in school?**
The Ape, B, C's.

*Jill Kerby*

**Where do horses go when they are sick?**
To the horspital.

*Sarah Breeyear*

**What kind of pig likes to drive a car?**
A road hog.

*Anthony Loeffler*

# Elephant Express

**Why do ducks have flat feet?**
To stamp out forest fires.
**Why do elephants have flat feet?**
To stamp out burning ducks.
*Lukas Plank*

**Who does an elephant call
when its toe hurts?**
A tow truck.
*Alison Reese*

**Why did the elephant sit on the
marshmallow?**
To keep from falling in the hot
chocolate.
*Taj Gibbs*

**How do you make an elephant float?**
Mix soda, syrup, ice cream and an elephant.
*Suzanne Pagliorola*

**Why do elephants have trunks?**
Because they would look silly carrying suitcases.
*Tina Rose*

**What did the grape do when the elephant sat on it?**
It let out a little whine.
*Tatum Ward*

**How do you know if an elephant used your toothbrush?**
It will smell like peanuts.
*Mikelle Fretz*

**If an elephant didn't have a trunk, how would he smell?**
Trunk or no trunk, he'd still smell terrible.
*Christine Palkovic*

**Why can't two elephants go swimming at the same time?**
Because they only have one pair of trunks.
*Jennifer Chambers*

**What time is it when five elephants run after one elephant?**
Five after one.
*Amanda Moore*

# Icky & Ooky

**Why did the fly fly?**
Because the spider spied her.
*Anne Shindel*

**What do you call spiders that get married?**
Newlywebs.
*Carrie Rentler*

**Do snakes need silverware when they eat?**
No, because they have forked tongues.
*Christi Dodd*

**What is a mosquito's favorite sport?**
Skin diving.
*Jaymi Bradford*

**Why was the insect kicked out of the forest?**
Because it was a litterbug.
*Elizabeth Burns*

**Why are snakes considered to be thrifty?**
Because they can make both ends meet.
*Kelly Coughlin*

**Why do spiders spin webs?**
Because they don't know how to knit.
*Erin Eickenhorst*

**Why do spiders make good baseball players?**
Because they know how to catch flies.
*Chris Pagleno*

**How does a bee comb its hair?**
With a honey comb.
*Cassie Lynne Peterson*

**What did the mama firefly say to the papa firefly?**
"Isn't Junior bright for his age?"
*Julie Schroeder*

**What is the first thing a snake learns in school?**
Hisss-tory.
*Elizabeth Noe*

# Ridiculous Riddles

**When is a car not a car?**
When it turns into a driveway.

Michael Johnson

**Why was six afraid of seven?**
Because seven, *ate,* nine.

Marci Healy

**What is black and white and read all over?**
A newspaper.

Tanya Mason

**How can you get 45 using only 4, 4, 4, and 4? You can't add, subtract, multiply or divide.**
44 $\frac{4}{4}$.

Lorraine Dorn

**What kind of music did the Pilgrims dance to?**
Plymouth Rock.

Willie Cartagera

**If two is a couple, and three is a crowd, what's four and five?**
Nine.

Donna Cusano

**If it took 20 minutes for one man to fill a bathtub with water using one bucket, how long will it take for two men with two buckets to fill the same bathtub?**
No time at all because the other man already filled it up.

Christie Cardarella

**What time is it when the clock strikes thirteen?**
Time to get a new clock.

Jason Chaney

**What runs but never moves, and has hands but can't hold anything?**
A clock.

Nathan Baird

**What is fog?**
A cloud that is afraid of heights.

*Heather Donn Morgan*

**As long as I eat I am fine. But when I drink, I die. What am I?**
A fire.

*Candice Vinson*

**What starts with T, ends with T, and is full of T?**
A teapot.

*Brandi Jones*

**What has feet and legs, but cannot walk?**
A pair of stockings.

*Crystal Dawn Akers*

**What has a head and a tail but no body?**
A coin.

*Kandi Hankins*

**Why is the nose in the middle of the face?**
Because it's the scenter.

*Benjamin Florez*

**What has one foot at each end and has a third foot in the middle?**
A yardstick.

*Ashley Muratori*

**Why do dragons sleep all day?**
Because they like to hunt knights.

*Jon Barnes*

**How many seconds are in a year?**
Twelve. There's January 2nd, February 2nd, March 2nd, April 2nd, May 2nd, June 2nd, July 2nd, August 2nd, September 2nd, October 2nd, November 2nd, and December 2nd.

*Tara Holland*

**Someone takes this and you don't know what it looks like. You have never seen it before, but when you get it back you know it is yours. What is it?**
Your picture.

*Marisa McRainey*

**What are the two strongest days of the week?**
Saturday and Sunday. The rest are weak days.

*Amy Kay Hudson*

# Kooky Knock-Knocks

Knock! Knock!
Who's there?
Osborne.
Osborne who?
Osborne in Texas, how about you?

*Nathaniel Hart-Benham*

Knock! Knock!
Who's there?
Eliza.
Eliza who?
Eliza lot, so don't believe him.
*Jerry Alexander*

Knock! Knock!
Who's there?
Heaven.
Heaven who?
Heaven you heard this before?
*Jessica Abler*

Knock! Knock!
Who's there?
Scold.
Scold who?
S'cold outside, let me in.

*Brian Poindexter*

Knock! Knock!
Who's there?
Catsup.
Catsup who?
Cats up a tree.
*Josh Lindsey*

Knock! Knock!
Who's there?
Whenna.
Whenna who?
Whenna you gonna let me in?

*Elizabeth Naylor*

Knock! Knock!
Who's there?
Zoom.
Zoom who?
Zoom do you expect?
*Heather Jordan*

Knock! Knock!
Who's there?
Amos.
Amos who?
Amosquito bit me.
Knock! Knock!
Who's there?
Andy.
Andy who?
Andy bit me again.

*Sarah Dowst*

Knock! Knock!
Who's there?
Canoe.
Canoe who?
Canoe come out and play with me?

*Nicole Condon*

# Vampires & Skeletons

**Why do vampires play cards at the cemetery?**
Because they can always dig up an extra player.

*Gregory Van Dyke*

**Why did the little vampires stay up all night?**
Because they were studying for a blood test.

*Jeff McMurray*

**What's a vampire's favorite fruit?**
A neck-tarine.

*Erich Zorn*

**What test did Dracula take before the movie?**
A scream test.

*Marc Vasher*

**Where does Dracula work?**
At the blood bank.

*Ami Tulin*

**What is Dracula's favorite dog?**
A bloodhound.

*Jennifer Bellizzi*

**What is Dracula's favorite flavor of ice cream?**
Vein-illa.

*Steven Cundiff*

**What did the vampire do at the art contest?**
He drew blood.

*Michael Bell*

**How many vampires does it take to change a light bulb?**
None. Vampires prefer the dark.

*Katy Decker*

**What does one angry skeleton say to another skeleton?**
"I've got a bone to pick with you."

*Albert Manuel*

**Why didn't the skeleton go to the ball?**
Because he didn't have any body to go with.

*Jeremy Christensen*

**Why don't vampires like sleeping people?**
Because they don't like tired blood.

*Charles Jones*

**Why did the skeleton go to the library?**
Because he wanted to bone up on a few things.

*Jason Higgerson*

**Why did the skeleton get such a high score on the quiz?**
Because it got the bone-us question.

*Kerriann Engholm*

**Why do vampires drink blood?**
Because root beer makes them burp.
*Kelly Nelson*

**Why do skeletons hate winter?**
Because the cold goes right through them.
*Heather Patrick*

**Why don't people like vampires?**
Because they're a pain in the neck.
*Mike Gonzales*

**What's as sharp as a vampire's fang?**
His other fang.

*Marlys Fassett*

**Who won the skeleton beauty contest?**
Nobody.

*Tammi Sramek*

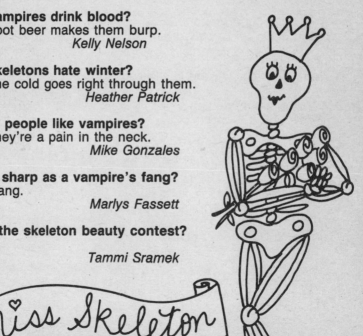

miss Skeleton

# Odds & Ends

**Where does the Lone Ranger take his trash?**
To the dump, to the dump, to the dump, dump, dump.

*David Dean*

**Why did the boy throw the letter out the window?**
Because he wanted to send it air mail.

*Chad Palmer*

**Why did the boy stand behind the donkey?**
Because he thought he would get a kick out of it.

*Ben Angley*

**What is the difference between a cat and a comma?**
One has claws at the end of its paws, and the other has a pause at the end of its clause.

*Jason Lee*

Ted: Call your dog off.
Karen: I can't. I've called him Muffin ever since he was a pup.

*Katrina Smolinski*

One day, a boy walked into a fish store and said, "Throw your four biggest fish into the air—fast!" When the manager asked why, the boy said, "So I can honestly tell my mom I caught them."

*Erin Harris*

**What should you do before you get off a bus?**
Let it stop.

*Jay Shipley*

Jill: What is the first letter in yellow?
Terry: Y.
Jill: Because I want to know.

*Jill Schultz*

Jennifer: Did you know it takes three sheep to make a sweater?
Dawn: I didn't even know sheep could knit.

*Joelle Proulx*

28

Kim: Have you ever seen a barn dance?
Tim: No, but I've seen a chimney sweep.

*Meghan Hicks*

John: I don't understand it. If your father bought your mother a mink, why is she so mad?
Jeff: Because she has to clean out its cage.

*John Hill*

Bobby: I know someone who thinks he's an owl.
Danny: Who?
Bobby: Now I know two.

*Jason Saniano*

First Passenger: Do these buses run on time?
Second Passenger: No, they run on wheels.

*Robert Young*

**How many months have 28 days in them?**
All of them!

*Melissa Musgrove*

**A man had two sons and named them both Ed. Why?**
Because two Eds are better than one.

*Nick Pakula*

There were three men on an island. One man found a genie bottle. The genie said that he would grant them three wishes. The first man wished to be home with his family, and then he was. The second man wished for the same, and he too was gone. The third man felt kind of lonely, and said, "I wish my two friends were back."

*Angela Barkley*

**Why did the boy put his father in the freezer?**
So he would get a "pop"cicle.

*Michelle Blocker*

Jamie: Did your watch stop when it dropped on the floor?
Wesley: Of course it did. Did you expect it to go right through?

*Jamie Knotts*

# Ghastly Ghouls

**Why don't ghosts like rain?**
Because it dampens their spirits.

*Jarrod Canepa*

**What happened when the girl ghost met the boy ghost?**
It was love at first fright.

*Viviana Alonz*

**Why did the ghost like disco dancing?**
Because it liked to boogie.

*Kelly Davis*

**How can you tell if a mummy has been in your refrigerator?**
The leftovers will be re-wrapped in bandages.

*Charles Brinck*

**What is the most important rule for witches?**
Don't fly off the handle!

*Katie Peterman*

**What did the mother ghost say to the junior ghost in the car?**
"Fasten your sheet belt."

*Erin Hunter*

**What's worse than a witch without a broom?**
A vampire with false teeth.

*Eric Person*

**What did one ghost say to the other ghost?**
"Do you believe in people?"

*Krishanna Mask*

**What did the witch ask for in the hotel?**
Broom service.

*Krista Dorsaneo*

**Where do ghosts like to swim?**
In the Dead Sea.

*Lorenzo Graham*

**How can you make a witch scratch?**
Take away the w and she'll itch.
*Cybrian Williams*

**Where do spirits mail their letters?**
At the ghost office.

*Nicole Fuller*

**What is a witch's favorite subject?**
Spelling.

*Edward Avallone*

**What did the mother ghost tell her little ghost?**
"Don't spook until you are spooken to."

*Kris Robertson*

**What kind of witch rides a golden broom?**
A rich witch.

*Tammy Burgess*

**What does a ghost like to eat for lunch?**
Booberry pie and I scream.

*Allison David*

**When do ghosts play baseball?**
When their spirit is catching.
*Kate Whiting*

**Why did the little ghost flunk his spelling test?**
Because he made too many boo-boo's.

*Danielle Carson*

**Why does a witch fly on a broom?**
So she won't be left in the dust.

*Mary Kelly Carter*

**Why did the mummy skip lunch?**
Because it was too wrapped up in its work.

*David Theriault*

# ...No Place Like Home

Young Man: Sir, I've come to ask for your daughter's hand in marriage.
Father: You'll have to take all of her or it's no deal.

*Gopal Sachdeva*

**What is the last thing you take off when you go to bed?**
You take your feet off the floor.

*Kristen Hutson*

Brother: I'm going to give Mom a beautiful cut-glass flower vase for her birthday.
Sister: But she already has a beautiful cut-glass flower vase.
Brother: No, she doesn't. I just dropped it.

*Brooke Jackman*

**Why did the little boy take his bike to bed with him?**
So he would not have to walk in his sleep.

*Shannon Oliver*

A mother and father were worried about their 5-year-old son. He never spoke a word in his life. One day at the breakfast table, the boy said, "Can I have some sugar on my cereal?" The mother and father were shocked and excited. The mother said to the boy, "Son, you can speak! Why haven't you ever said anything up till now?" The boy shrugged, and said, "Up till now, everything has been okay."

*Marta deCandia*

**Why did the boy close his eyes when he looked in the mirror?**
Because he wanted to see what he looked like when he was sleeping.

*Stephanie Hall*

(Suzie's teacher knocked on the door to her house.)
Teacher: Suzie, is your mother here?
Suzie: Nope, she ain't.
Teacher: Suzie, your grammar!
Suzie: She ain't here either.

*Kim Humphries*

**Why did the boy disconnect his doorbell?**
Because he wanted to win the "No-bell" Prize.
*Sandi Krenz*

# Farm-Fresh Funnies

City Visitor: Look at that bunch of cows.
Farmer: Herd.
City Visitor: Heard of what?
Farmer: Herd of cows.
City Visitor: Sure! I've heard of cows.

*Justin Stark*

**What did the cherry tree say to the farmer?**
"Stop picking on me."

*Dareece Williams*

**When is a chicken most likely to go into the hen house?**
When the door is open.

*Sonja Daniels*

**What did the cow ask the silo?**
"Is my fodder in there?"

*Mark Matson*

**Why do baby pigs eat so much?**
Because they want to make hogs of themselves.

*Naomi Caudle*

**Why did the farmer go over the potato crop with such a heavy roller?**
Because he wanted to grow mashed potatoes.

*Nathan Peterson*

**Why was the farmer so famous?**
Because he was out standing in his field.

*Joann Metz*

**Why don't farmers tell secrets on the farm?**
Because the corn has ears, the potatoes have eyes, and the beans talk.

*Lori Dubach*

**What should you do if a chicken lays a golden egg?**
Tell it to lay more.

*Kaiesha Flucas*

**What did the chick say to the other chick when the hen laid an orange instead of an egg?**
"Look at the orange marmalade."

*Joshua White*

33

# Down by the Sea

**What did the girl octopus say to the boy octopus?**
"I want to hold your hand, hand, hand, hand, hand, hand, hand, hand."

*Lindsey Fillman*

**How do you correspond with a fish?**
Drop it a line.

*Sara Collett*

**Where do fish keep their money?**
In the river bank.

*Erica Neri*

**How does an octopus go into battle?**
Well-armed.

*Lisa Williams*

**Why are fish so smart?**
Because they swim in schools.

*Misty Jones*

**Where does a fish sleep?**
In a water bed.

*Chris Courchesne*

**What should you feed your pet frog?**
Croakers and milk.

*Timothy Cook*

**Why don't sea gulls ever fly across the bay?**
Because then they would be bagels.

*Jessica Mazella*

**What does a frog order at a snack bar?**
French flies and a large croak.

*Stephanie Munsterman*

**When does a duck wake up?**
At the quack of dawn.

*Allison Rudig*

**Why are baby tadpoles the best storytellers?**
Because older frogs have lost their tales.

*Katie Hillman*

# Off to Work We Go

**Why did the man get fired from the orange juice factory?**
Because he couldn't concentrate.

*Amy Tolliver*

**How does an auctioneer look when conducting a sale?**
For-bidding.

*George Remus*

**What is the most useless invention?**
A solar-powered flashlight.

*David Ure*

**Why did the man wear boxing gloves on the freeway?**
To fight the traffic.

*Shaila Nevarez*

**When are cooks mean?**
When they beat the eggs and whip the cream.

*James Kearns*

**If a king sits on gold, who sits on silver?**
The Lone Ranger.

*Rachel Kitzman*

**Why does a candlemaker have it easy?**
Because he only works on wick ends.

*Derek Brown*

**What's the worst season of the year for a tightrope walker?**
The fall.

*Renee Southward*

**Why did the audience throw eggs at the actor?**
Because ham and eggs go well together.

*Cindy Crans*

**What does a baseball player do when he gets hot?**
He stands in front of the fans.

*Christy Tincher*

# Snicker Doodles

**What part does a lion have in a play?**
The mane part.

*Kelly O'Connor*

**What time is it after dinner?**
Ate o'clock.

*Sarah Holmboe*

**If an airplane crashed on the border of the United States and Canada, where would you bury the survivors?**
Nowhere. You don't bury survivors.

*Daniel Hale*

**From what number can you take away half, and get nothing?**
8. Take away the top half and you have 0.

*Colleen Flanigan*

**If it's raining cats and dogs, what might you step in?**
A poodle.

*Daniel Dezinski*

**How can you double your money?**
Put it in front of a mirror.

*Corey Williams*

**What can you sit on, sleep on, and brush your teeth with?**
A chair, a bed, and a toothbrush.

*Meghan Holston*

**What kind of table has no legs?**
A multiplication table.

*Leigh Dunnam*

**How can you tell if a volcano is mad?**
It will blow its top.

*Jamie Parker*

**When does water stop running downhill?**
When it gets to the bottom, of course!

*Scott Helmbrecht*

**What was the longest line at the joker's party?**
The punch line.

*Erin Costanzo*

**What is the hottest day of the week?**
Friday.

*Beth Williams*


**What's easy to get into, but hard to get out of?**
Trouble.

*Jeffrey Carter*


**Why would most dogs make good archaeologists?**
Because they like digging up old bones.

*Joey Libby*


**Can two three-month-old dogs fall for each other?**
Sure! But it'll only be puppy love.

*Sabrina Rojas*


**What did the dog in the Old West say when it limped into town?**
"I'm lookin' for the varmint who shot my paw."

*Beth Ann Sinclair*


Sue: What is your dog's name?
Dan: Ginger.
Sue: Does Ginger bite?
Dan: No, Ginger snaps.

*Jennifer Brierley*


Passenger: Is this my train?
Conductor: No, sir. It belongs to the railroad company.

*Sara Smith*


There once was a lady who married four men—a banker, an actor, a hairdresser, and an undertaker. One day a man asked why she married four men. She said, "One for the money, two for the show, three to get ready, and four to go."

*Jody Fleury*


**What did the judge say when the skunk sprayed the court?**
"Odor in the court."

*Laura Houde*

Mary: Will you always remember me?
Lou: Always.
Mary: Knock! Knock!
Lou: Who's there?
Mary: How could you forget me so soon?
*Christopher Barrosse*

# Neighborhood Nonsense

**Why did the girl sit on her watch?**
Because she wanted to be on time.

*Corinne Rios*

**If the red house is on the south side of the street, and the blue house is on the north side of the street, where is the White House?**
In Washington, D.C.

*Christina Butler*

**What's worse than raining cats and dogs?**
Hailing taxis.

*Angela Huff*

**What can go up the chimney down, but cannot go down the chimney up?**
An umbrella.

*Aaron Borling*

**How do leaves change in the fall?**
Autumn-atically.

*Jennifer Nahrebeski*

**Why do tea kettles whistle?**
Because they never learned to sing.
*Thomas Fraser*

**Why do traffic signals turn red?**
You would too if you had to change in public.
*Dina Sireika*

**Why did the old lady put roller skates on her rocking chair?**
Because she wanted to rock and roll.

*Heather Franck*

**Why did the man put the clock under his pillow?**
Because he wanted to sleep over time.
*Misty Brown*

**What kind of dress do you have, but never wear?**
Your address.

*Jennifer Goric*

**Charlie Buckner is a butcher. He has 20/20 vision, hears real well, and is very smart. What does he weigh?**
Meat.

*Elisa Ramos*

**What is the tallest building in New York City?**
The library, because it has the most stories.

*Nate Stulman*

Ron: Where are you going with that watering can?
Don: To water the flowers.
Ron: But it's raining outside.
Don: That's okay, I have my raincoat on.

*Cody Pitts*

Tim: Did you hear about the big fight on the train last night?
Bill: No, what happened.
Tim: The conductor punched a ticket.

*Jenny Scott*

John and Mike had a table stuck in the doorway. After about 20 minutes, John said, "This table sure is hard to get in." "Get in?" asked Mike. "I've been pushing it out."

*Debbie Jo Dolansky*

**Why did Jennifer go out with her purse open?**
Because she was expecting some change in the weather.

*Ryan P. Dunn*

Boy: You should keep your eyes open tomorrow.
Girl: Why?
Boy: Because if you don't, you might bump into something.

*Laura Mico-Monaco*

Susan: Do you have holes in your socks?
Jennifer: No.
Susan: Then how do you get your feet in?

*Jessica Mary Selander*

Bill: This match won't light.
Jim: What's the matter with it?
Bill: I don't know. It worked great a minute ago!

*Shawn Schnell*

Customer: I would like these nails, please.
Clerk: That will be 59 cents plus tax.
Customer: I don't want tacks, just nails.

*Kelley Dooley*

# Fun! Fun! Funny!

Teacher: Bobby, you were late for school this morning, you were late yesterday, and you were late the day before that. What is the matter?

Bobby: I can't help it. I run down Main Street every day. Then I come to a sign that says "SCHOOL - GO SLOW." So I do!

*Elizabeth Smith*

**If one boy has 9 piles of hay, and another has 21 piles of hay, how many piles of hay do they have altogether?**
One.

*James Svesnik*

**If all the letters of the alphabet were invited to a tea party, what letters would be late?**
The letters U, V, W, X, Y and Z, because they all come after T.

*Lori Harms*

**What has 6 legs, 4 ears, 4 eyes, 1 tail, 2 mouths, and 2 noses?**
A man riding a horse.

*Raymond A.C. White*

**What part of a fish weighs the most?**
The scales.

*Tina Pappas*

40

Mother: What did you learn in school today?
Daughter: Not enough. I have to go back tomorrow.

*Tammie Davis*

**Why did the man put bandages on his refrigerator?**
Because it had cold cuts.

*Lisa Huddleston*

**What makes more noise than one squealing pig?**
Two squealing pigs.

*Gail McKinney*

**What kind of truck do farmers take their pigs to market in?**
In a pig up truck.

*Natalie Gillespie*

Barb: Which hand do you stir your cocoa with?
Ben: Neither, I use a spoon.

*Brandy Broussard*

**Why did the boy stand on his head?**
Because he was trying to turn things over in his mind.

*Quincy D. Edison*

**What has four wheels and flies?**
A garbage truck.

*Rachel Gibbs*

# A Special Thanks To:

Abler, Jessica, 8, Sacred Heart School, Norfolk, NE
Acreman, Sandy, 10, Dunbar Elem., Ramer, AL
Aguirre, Maria, 8, L.K. Hall Elem., Dallas, TX
Akers, Crystal Dawn, Grade 4, Booker T. Washington School, Lexington, KY
Alexander, Jerry, 11, York School, Springfield, MO
Alonz, Viviana, 8, St. Anselm School, Bronx, NY
Angley, Ben, 7, Flint River Academy, Woodbury, GA
Arbour, Tommy, 11, Our Lady of Mercy School, Baton Rouge, LA
Arrigo, Andrea, 10, St. Clare School, Staten Island, NY
Avallone, Edward, 8, Saint Stephen School, Hamden, CT
Bainter, Raquelle, 10, Hoxie Grade School, Hoxie, KS
Baird, Nathan, Grade 1, Indianapolis Public School No. 61, Indianapolis, IN
Baldwin, Emily, 8, P.S. 87 Manhattan, New York, NY
Barb, Jeremy, 11, Triplett Middle, Mount Jackson, VA
Barkley, Angela, 10, Clover Middle, Clover, SC
Barnes, Jon, 7, Lincolnview East Elem., Middle Point, OH
Barrosse, Christopher, 8, Our Lady Star of the Sea School, New Orleans, LA
Beier, Carmen, 12, Our Savior Lutheran School, Fenton, MO
Bell, Michael, 8, Hagerstown Elem., Hagerstown, IN
Bellizzi, Jennifer, 8, Eli Whitney School, Stratford, CT
Bernotus, Craig, 8, Timothy Ball Elem., Crown Point, IN
Bledsoe, Rebecca, 9, Fair Grove School, Thomasville, NC
Blocker, Michelle, 11, Holland Hall School, Tulsa, OK
Boemi, Nicole, 10, St. Clare School, Staten Island, NY
Bonarigo, David, 11, Liberty School, Orland Park, IL
Borling, Aaron, 11, Liberty School, Orland Park, IL
Bowen, Christine, 9, Balboa Street Magnet School, Northridge, CA
Bradford, Jaymi, 9, Fair Grove School, Thomasville, NC
Breeyear, Sarah, 8, Grand Isle Elem., Grand Isle, VT
Brierley, Jennifer, 7, Lonsdale Elem., Lincoln, RI
Brinck, Charles, 9, Paulding Elem., Paulding, OH
Broussard, Brandy, 11, Our Lady of Mercy School, Baton Rouge, LA
Brown, Chris, 6, Carolyn Wenz School, Paris, IL
Brown, Derek, 10, Tinicum Elem., Pipersville, PA
Brown, Misty, 10, MGM School, Farrell, PA

Bryson, Wendy, Grade 2, Wetumpka Elem., Wetumpka, AL
Bullock, April Bree, 11, Collins Middle, Collins, MS
Bulthuis, Brandon, 7, Wheatfield Elem., Wheatfield, IN
Burgess, Tammy, 9, Wernert Elem., Toledo, OH
Burns, Elizabeth, 9, Pinecrest School, Greenwood, SC
Butala, Mike, 8, Bartman Elem., Hermitage, PA
Butler, Christina, 5, Carolyn Wenz School, Paris, IL
Callan, Katie, 8, Carlisle Elem., Carlisle, IA
Campanaro, Jenny, 8, Spring Garden Elem., Bedford, TX
Campbell, Tara, 8, Manchester Elem., Manchester, KY
Canepa, Jarrod, 10, St. Clare School, Staten Island, NY
Cardarella, Christie, 10, Henry Barnard School, Enfield, CT
Caris, Stacie, 10, W.H. Rhodes Elem., Milton, FL
Carson, Danielle, 7, Fairview Elem., Mora, MN
Cartagera, Willie, 9, Joel School, Clinton, CT
Carter, Jeffrey, 7, Lincoln Park Elem., Knoxville, TN
Carter, Mary Kelly, 9, Seven Oaks Elem., Columbia, SC
Caudle, Naomi, 10, W.H. Rhodes Elem., Milton, FL
Chambers, Jennifer, 7, Piedmont Elem., Dandridge, TN
Chandiramani, Rachna, 10, Gateway Upper Elem., Monroeville, PA
Chaney, Jason, 8, Hagerstown Elem., Hagerstown, IN
Charles, Andrea, 7, Ramon C. Cobbs Lower, Newark, DE
Christensen, Jeremy, 9, Johnson Elem., Mesa, AZ
Church, Amanda, Grade 3, Central Elem., Clinton, IN
Ciregna, Steven, 9, St. Athanasius School, Brooklyn, NY
Collett, Sara, 6, Coral Springs Elem., Coral Springs, FL
Condon, Nicole, 8, Highlands Elem., Wilmington, DE
Connors, Cheryl, 10, St. Benedict Joseph Labre School,
   Richmond Hill, NY
Cook, Timothy, 11, Houston Middle, Houston, MS
Costanzo, Erin, 11, St. Odilia School, Shoreview, MN
Coughlin, Kelly, 8, Orange Avenue School, Cranford, NJ
Courchesne, Chris, 7, Veterans Park School, Ludlow, MA
Crans, Cindy, 11, Our Lady of Mount Carmel School, Boonton, NJ
Cumberland, Amanda, 8, Ricardo Elem., Kingsville, TX
Cunat, Jimmy, 9, Liberty School, Orland Park, IL
Cundiff, Steven, 10, Lincoln School, Bedford, IN
Cusano, Donna, 8, Saint Stephen School, Hamden, CT
Dagostino, Lucilla, 10, Hampton School, Hampton, NJ
Daniels, Sonja, 9, 60th Street School, Niagara Falls, NY
Darby, Ronald, 9, Manchester School, Windham, ME
Dattilio, Erica, 7, Paramount School, Hagerstown, MD
David, Allison, 9, Norton Elem., Snellville, GA
Davis, Kelly, 11, Littleton Elem., Cashion, AZ
Davis, Tammie, 9, Gandy Elem., White Hall, AR
Day, Eric, 8, Highlands Elem., Wilmington, DE
Dean, David, 11, Demarest Elem., Demarest, GA
deCandia, Marta, 8, Robert L. Craig School, Moonachie, NJ
Decker, Katy, Grade 4, Our Lady Of Lourdes, Hitchcock, TX
DeLaire, Nichole, 8, Our Lady Czestochowa School, Coventry, RI
DeLano, Stephanie, 10, Kramer Middle, Willimantic, CT
Denlinger, Tommie, 8, Paradise Elem., Paradise, PA
Dezinski, Daniel, 9, Crescentwood School, East Detroit, MI

DiNardo, Erik, 6, Cedar Hill School, Towaco, NJ
Dodd, Christi, 9, Howe Valley School, Cecilia, KY
Dolansky, Debbie Jo, 8, St. Elizabeth Elem., Pittsburgh, PA
Dooley, Kelley, 11, St. Odilia School, Shoreview, MN
Dorn, Lorraine, 9, Southwood Elem., Old Bridge, NJ
Dorsaneo, Krista, 10, St. Callistus School, Philadelphia, PA
Dowst, Sarah, 10, Old County Road School, Esmond, RI
Dubach, Lori, 11, Geneva Elem., Geneva, IN
Dunn, Ryan P., 11, Our Lady of Mount Carmel School, Boonton, NJ
Dunnam, Leigh, 8, St. Pius X School, Mobile, AL
Edison, Quincy D., Grade 4, Booker T. Washington School,
   Lexington, KY
Eickenhorst, Erin, 7, Nathan Hale School, Manchester, CT
Enderby, Matt, 6, Lincolnview East Elem., Middle Point, OH
Engholm, Kerrlann, 10, St. Odilia School, Shoreview, MN
Esposito, Lauren, 7, Alburtis School, Alburtis, PA
Evanush, Nikki, 9, Bonny Kate School, Knoxville, TN
Falkner, Haddi, 7, Bartman Elem., Hermitage, PA
Farries, Rachelle, 9, Hueytown Elem., Hueytown, AL
Fassett, Marlys, 9, Morgan School, Beloit, WI
Feulner, Jason, 8, Severn School, Corning, NY
Fike, Joy, 9, Bradford Elem., Bradford, OH
Fillman, Lindsey, 8, Ramon C. Cobbs Lower, Newark, DE
Flanigan, Colleen, 10, St. Michael School, Livonia, MI
Fleury, Jody, 8, Brewerton Elem., Brewerton, NY
Florez, Benjamin, 7, Noble Elem., Cleveland Heights, OH
Flucas, Kaiesha, 9, L.L. Hotchkiss Montessori Academy, Dallas, TX
Fraerman, Andrew, 6, South School, Glenco, IL
Franck, Heather, 9, St. Johns Lutheran School, Napa, CA
Fraser, Thomas, 9, St. Clare School, Staten Island, NY
Frederickson, Penny, 8, Wakefield Elem., Wakefield, NE
Fretz, Mikelle, 7, Liberty School, Scottsdale, AZ
Friese, Laura, 10, Flanagan Jr. High, Flanagan, IL
Frohnheiser, Lisa, 10, St. Anne School, Bethlehem, PA
Fry, Wendy, 7, Wheatfield Elem., Wheatfield, IN
Fuller, Nicole, 8, Westside Elem., Daytona Beach, FL
Furnival, Jodi, 8, Park School, Munhall, PA
Galati, Vanessa, 8, Deer Park Avenue Elem., North Babylon, NY
Gallagher, Jessicah, 7, McNair School, Hazelwood, MO
Garrett, Billy, 10, Lynn Kirk Elem., Youngstown, OH
Garrison, Cindy, 10, Opdyke Grade School, Opdyke, IL
Gibbs, Rachel, 10, Peavine School, Reno, NV
Gibbs, Taj, Grade 3, Pine Lake Elem., Miami, FL
Gillespie, Natalie, 10, Tazewell Elem., Tazewell, VA
Gobel, April, 7, Andover Elem., Andover, KS
Gonzales, Mike, 9, Mitchell Elem., Racine, WI
Goric, Jennifer, 8, Windmere School, Ellington, CT
Graham, Lorenzo, 10, MGM School, Farrell, PA
Greening, Erin, 9, Liberty School, Orland Park, IL
Hale, Daniel, 10, St. Michael School, Livonia, MI
Hall, Denece, 9, Palm Vista Elem., 29 Palms, CA
Hall, Stephanie, 11, Bondurant Middle, Frankfort, KY
Hallowell, Jesse, 10, Tinicum Elem., Pipersville, PA

Hankins, Kandi, 7, Ajo Elem., Ajo, AZ
Harms, Lori, 10, Flanagan Jr. High, Flanagan, IL
Harris, Erin, 11, Blackburn Elem., Independence, MO
Harris, Marquist, 9, Jimmy Brown Elem., Star City, AR
Harrison, Liam E., 9, Gayhead Elem., Hopewell Junction, NY
Hart-Benham, Nathaniel, 10, John F. Long Elem., Phoenix, AZ
Healy, Marci, 11, Blessed Trinity School, Ocala, FL
Heineke, Amy, 9, Morgan School, Beloit, WI
Helmbrecht, Scott, 8, Fairview Elem., Mora, MN
Hicks, Meghan, 10, St. Odilia School, Shoreview, MN
Higgerson, Jason, 8, McNair School, Hazelwood, MO
Hill, John, 8, Newport Elem., Newport, NC
Hillman, Katie, 8, Lenox School, Portland, OR
Hines, Robert, Grade 2, University Lab School, Baton Rouge, LA
Holland, Tara, 9, Augusta Christian School, Martinez, GA
Holmboe, Sarah, 8, Orchard Hills School, Novi, MI
Holston, Meghan, 9, St. Pius X School, Mobile, AL
Horvath, Ryan, 8, Liberty School, Scottsdale, AZ
Houde, Laura, 8, Towpath School, Avon, CT
Hoy, Bryan, 7, Prides Corner School, Westbrook, ME
Huddleston, Lisa, 9, Gandy Elem., White Hall, AR
Hudson, Amy Kay, 11, Doyle-Ryder School, Flint, MI
Huff, Angela, 11, Oak Grove West School, Bartonville, IL
Humphries, Kim, 11, Bluestem Middle, Leon, KS
Hunter, Cindy, 10, McKinley School, Huron, SD
Hunter, Erin, 8, Orchard Hill Farm School, Tinley Park, IL
Hushagen, Danny, 7, Fairview Elem., Mora, MN
Hutson, Kristen, 9, North Elem., Marshall, IL
Jackman, Brooke, 10, Vernon Middle, East Norwich, NY
Johnson, Michael, 9, St. Andrew School, Orlando, FL
Johnston, Megan, 7, Park School, Munhall, PA
Jones, Brandi, 11, Meadowview Elem., Bossier City, LA
Jones, Charles, 10, Beck Elem., Columbus, OH
Jones, Derron, Grade 4, Booker T. Washington School, Lexington, KY
Jones, Misty, 9, Hueytown Elem., Hueytown, AL
Jordan, Heather, 6, Prides Corner School, Westbrook, ME
Kearns, James, 8, Liberty School, Scottsdale, AZ
Kendrick, Jonathan, Grade 2, University Lab School, Baton Rouge, LA
Kerby, Jill, 8, Spencer Elem., Spencer, WV
Kitzman, Rachel, 9, Converse School, Beloit, WI
Knotts, Jamie, 10, Flemington Elem., Flemington, WV
Kobolt, Holly, 11, Eastgate Middle, Kansas City, MO
Krenz, Sandi, 10, St. Odilia School, Shoreview, MN
Kubczak, Leah, 7, Erskine School, Cedar Rapids, IA
Lantz, Megan, 9, Pine Butte Elem., Colstrip, MT
Lee, Jason, 9, Augusta Christian School, Martinez, GA
Lee, Travis, 10, Walnut School, Chino, CA
Libby, Joey, 10, 60th Street School, Niagara Falls, NY
Lieb, Brenda, 7, Penns Manor Elem., Clymer, PA
Lindsey, Josh, 8, Fouke Elem., Fouke, AR
Link, Theresa, 8, St. Francis Xavier School, Cresson, PA
Lloyd, Sarah, 10, Wimbledon Courtenay School, Wimbledon, ND
Loeffler, Anthony, 9, Carl Sandburg Elem., Littleton, CO

Madonna, Allison, 7, Villa Maria Academy Lower, Immaculata, PA
Malaythong, David, Grade 1, Nevada Community School, Nevada, IA
Mangabang, Aaron, 11, Mary Immaculate School, Farmers Branch, TX
Manuel, Albert, 7, Ajo Elem., Ajo, AZ
Mask, Krishanna, 7, Howe Avenue School, Sacramento, CA
Mason, Tanya, 10, W.H. Rhodes Elem., Milton, FL
Matson, Mark, Grade 2, Vineland Elem., Rotunda West, FL
Mazella, Jessica, 10, St. Clare School, Staten Island, NY
McAuliffe, Kristen, 9, Kingston Elem., Kingston, MA
McCleary, Charley, 8, Windmere School, Ellington, CT
McClendon, Matt, 7, South Euless Elem., Euless, TX
McCracken, Erin, 7, Stoneleigh Elem., Baltimore, MD
McCulken, Christine, 10, St. Callistus School, Philadelphia, PA
McGovern, Kristy, 9, St. Thela School, Chicago, IL
McKinney, Gail, Grade 5, Morgantown Elem., Morgantown, KY
McMurray, Jeff, 9, Palm Vista Elem., 29 Palms, CA
McRainey, Marisa, 9, King Springs Elem., Smyrna, GA
Mertz, Jennifer, 9, Richland Elem., Quakertown, PA
Metz, Joann, 8, Crothersville Elem., Crothersville, IN
Mico-Monaco, Laura, 9, Van Sciver School, Haddonfield, NJ
Miller, Rusty, 8, Flint River Academy, Woodbury, GA
Minster, Sara, 9, Walnut School, Chino, CA
Molesky, Joseph, 9, Cherry Elem., Iron, MN
Molinares, Jessica, 10, St. Benedict Joseph Labre School,
    Richmond Hill, NY
Moore, Amanda, 7, R. Elisabeth Maclary Primary, Newark, DE
Moore, Conor, 7, Nathan Hale School, Manchester, CT
Morales, Nathan, 9, Foley Elem., Foley, AL
Morgan, Heather Donn, 8, Jefferson Elem., Jefferson, TX
Moser, Anna, 10, South Jordan Elem., South Jordan, UT
Moyer, Donald, 7, R. Elisabeth Maclary Primary, Newark, DE
Munsterman, Stephanie, 7, Southeast School, Clinton, MO
Muratori, Ashley, 8, St. Mary School, Sandusky, OH
Murphy, Patrick, 8, Tualatin Elem., Tualatin, OR
Musgrove, Melissa, 9, Gandy Elem., White Hall, AR
Muskie, Dan, 11, St. Francis of Assisi School, Springfield, PA
Nahrebeski, Jennifer, 11, McKinley Intermediate, Lackawanna, NY
Naylor, Elizabeth, 8, Hayward Elem., Hayward, WI
Nelson, Kelly, 8, Cherry Elem., Iron, MN
Neri, Erica, 7, A.H. Rockwell School, Bethel, CT
Nevarez, Shaila, 8, Waggoner School, Winters, CA
Nieken, Danny, 8, Wheatfield Elem., Wheatfield, IN
Noe, Elizabeth, 10, Gandy Elem., White Hall, AR
Norman, Tonetta, 11, P.S. 103, Bronx, NY
O'Connor, Kelly, 9, Liberty School, Orland Park, IL
Oliver, Shannon, 7, Camden Elem., Camden, NY
Pagleno, Chris, 10, Reid Elem., Athens, AL
Pagliorola, Suzanne, 5, River Plaza School, Red Bank, NJ
Pakula, Nick, 7, Corpus Christi School, Milwaukee, WI
Palkovic, Christine, 9, Lynn Kirk Elem., Youngstown, OH
Palmer, Chad, 8, Falling Creek Elem., Elberton, GA
Pappas, Tina, 9, Roosevelt School, Peru, IL
Parker, Jamie, 9, Andover Elem., Andover, KS
Patrick, Heather, 6, Wallace Elem., Bristol, VA

Payne, Tricia Lynn, 8, J.F. Gauthier Elem., St. Bernard, LA
Pecson, Lorena S., 10, Washington Elem., Hawthorne, CA
Person, Eric, 9, Liberty School, Orland Park, IL
Peterman, Katie, 8, Elsie C. Johnson School, Hanover Park, IL
Peterson, Cassie Lynne, Grade 2, E.N. Nordgaard Elem., Glenwood, MN
Peterson, Nathan, 8, Carlisle Elem., Carlisle, IA
Pitts, Cody, 9, Bauer-Speck School, Paso Robles, CA
Plank, Lukas, 9, Lake Placid Elem., Lake Placid, NY
Plata, Rocio, 8, L.K. Hall Elem., Dallas, TX
Podobinski, AnnMarie, 11, St. Odilia School, Shoreview, MN
Poindexter, Brian, 9, Jimmy Brown Elem., Star City, AR
Powers, Gary, 9, Tygart School, Parkersburg, WV
Proulx, Joelle, 8, Charlton Street School, Southbridge, MA
Pruitt, Brian, 11, O.P. Earle Elem., Landrum, SC
Puffer, Thomas Richard, 6, Hitchcock Elem., Hitchcock, SD
Ramos, Elisa, 11, Meadowview Elem., Bossier City, LA
Reding, David, 10, Palm Vista Elem., 29 Palms, CA
Reese, Alison, 9, Martin Luther King, Jr. Elem., Wilmington, DE
Remus, George, 8, St. John of the Cross School, Western Springs, IL
Rentler, Carrie, 7, Nathan Hale School, Manchester, CT
Rios, Corinne, 10, Busansky School, Pemberton, NJ
Rivenburg, Stacey, 9, Maine Memorial School, Maine, NY
Rivera, Michael, 11, Public School #4, Cliffside Park, NJ
Robertson, Kris, 10, Higgins Intermediate, Whitehouse, TX
Rogde, Allison, 8, Raguet Elem., Nacogdoches, TX
Rojas, Sabrina, 10, Bobby Duke Middle, Coachella, CA
Rose, Tina, 10, Sycamore School, Kokomo, IN
Rudig, Allison, 8, Tualatin Elem., Tualatin, OR
Russell, Marlena, 9, Fremont Older School, Cupertino, CA
Sachdeva, Gopal, 10, St. Benedict Joseph Labre School,
   Richmond Hill, NY
Sadowski, Tabitha, 8, Bartman Elem., Hermitage, PA
Saniano, Jason, 9, Western Branch Elem., Chesapeake, VA
Santoli, Anthony, 7, School No. 10, Belleville, NJ
Santone, Nicholas, 9, St. Callistus School, Philadelphia, PA
Scheffy, Rebecca, Grade 2, University Lab School, Baton Rouge, LA
Schmelzer, Jessica, 10, Clyde Erwin Flem., Jacksonville, NC
Schnell, Shawn, 9, Riveredge Elem., Berea, OH
Schroeder, Julie, 9, Wakefield Elem., Wakefield, NE
Schultz, Jill, 8, Minot Forest School, Wareham, MA
Scott, Jenny, 10, Grand Terrace Elem., Colton, CA
Selander, Jessica Mary, 9, Eli Whitney School, Stratford, CT
Sheehan, Joshua M., 9, John F. Long Elem., Phoenix, AZ
Shelton, Jason, 10, W.H. Rhodes Elem., Milton, FL
Shindel, Anne, 7, Hayshire Elem., York, PA
Shipley, Jay, 11, York School, Springfield, MO
Siewert, Shane, 9, Pine Butte Elem., Colstrip, MT
Sinclair, Beth Ann, 7, Glendale Elem., Flinton, PA
Sireika, Dina, 11, McKinley Intermediate, Lackawanna, NY
Sloan, Josh, 8, Carlisle Elem., Carlisle, IA
Smith, Elizabeth, 7, Lonsdale Elem., Lincoln, RI
Smith, Grady Allen, 11, Augusta Raa Middle, Tallahassee, FL
Smith, Sara, 11, Opdyke Grade School, Opdyke, IL
Smith, Thomas, 9, Fremont Older School, Cupertino, CA

Smolinski, Katrina, 10, Freeland Elem., Freeland, MI
Smythe, John, 11, Riccardi Elem., Glasco, NY
Southward, Renee, 9, Woodbury Elem., Woodbury, MN
Spitzer, Bradley, 7, Big Hollow School, Ingleside, IL
Sprouse, Jennifer, 8, Carlisle Elem., Carlisle, IA
Sramek, Tammi, Grade 5, Brooks School, Lewistown, MT
Stark, Justin, 8, Deer Park Avenue Elem., North Babylon, NY
Stewert, Kimberly, 6, Hilltop School, Caribou, ME
Stombres, Stefanie, 8, Kaneland Elem., Maple Park, IL
Strait, Taylor, 9, Seven Oaks Elem., Columbia, SC
Stulman, Nate, 9, Bigelow Hill School, Findlay, OH
Sunny, James, 10, Galena Middle, Galena, IL
Svesnik, James, Grade 4, West Hempfield Elem., Irwin, PA
Symonds, Andy, 9, Palm Vista Elem., 29 Palms, CA
Taylor, Angie, 7, Wickford Elem., North Kingstown, RI
Theriault, David, 7, Prides Corner School, Westbrook, ME
Tincher, Christy, 9, Custer School, Broken Bow, NE
Tindall, Matt, 7, Dawkins Middle, Spartanburg, SC
Tolliver, Amy, 5, Grove Elem., Montrose, IL
Tolman, Joleen, 8, Charlton Street School, Southbridge, MA
Tucci, Jennifer, 9, All Saints School, Pottsville, PA
Tulin, Ami, 10, Kramer Middle, Willimantic, CT
Twomey, Kevin, 10, St. Michael School, Livonia, MI
Tycer, Haley Dean, 9, Lewis Vincent Elem., Denham Springs, LA
Ure, David, 6, South School, Glenco, IL
van der Linde, Jason, 11, Our Savior Lutheran School, Fenton, MO
Van Dyke, Gregory, 8, T.R. Elem., Oyster Bay, NY
Vasher, Marc, 7, Vineland Elem., Rotunda West, FL
Vinson, Candice, 7, North Elem., Breckenridge, TX
Wang, Judy, 7, R. Elisabeth Maclary Primary, Newark, DE
Ward, Tatum, 11, Sycamore School, Kokomo, IN
Warmouth, Jennifer, 9, Lynn Kirk Elem., Youngstown, OH
Wasilchuk, Libby, 11, Vernon Middle, East Norwich, NY
White, Joshua, 9, Lexington Elem., Monroe, LA
White, Raymond A.C., 8, Saipan Community School, Saipan, MP
Whiting, Kate, 8, Lake Park School, Albany, GA
Williams, Beth, 7, Hopkins Elem., Richmond, VA
Williams, Corey, 8, Shades Mountain School, Birmingham, AL
Williams, Cybrian, 9, Opa Locka Elem., Opa Locka, FL
Williams, Dareece, 8, P.S. 250, Brooklyn, NY
Williams, Lisa, 11, Howe Valley School, Cecilia, KY
Williams, Matthew, 8, Log Pile School, Washington, PA
Wilson, Cindy, Grade 2, South Cumberland Elem., Crossville, TN
Winkel, Robert, 7, Judson School, Watertown, CT
Winston, Elisha, 10, C.G. Credle School, Oxford, NC
Wood, Kathryn, 10, St. Michael School, Livonia, MI
Wootton, Jason, 7, R. Elisabeth Maclary Primary, Newark, DE
Wright, Daniel, 9, P.J. Hill School, Trenton, NJ
Wyatt, Brandi, Grade 2, South Cumberland Elem., Crossville, TN
Young, Jonas, Grade 1, Indianapolis Public School No. 61,
   Indianapolis, IN
Young, Robert, 9, Jimmy Brown Elem., Star City, AR
Zorn, Erich, 8, Bon Meade Elem., Coraopolis, PA